W9-BCC-913

Greystone Books
A division of Douglas & McIntyre Ltd.
2323 Quebec Street, Suite 201
Vancouver, British Columbia
Canada V5T 4S7
www.greystonebooks.com

National Library of Canada Cataloguing in Publication Data
Rossiter, Sean, 1946–
    Mario Lemieux
    (Hockey heroes)

ISBN 1-55054-870-0

1. Lemieux, Mario, 1965– —Juvenile literature.
2. Hockey players—Canada—Biography—Juvenile literature.
I. Title II. Series: Hockey heroes (Vancouver, B.C.)

GV848.5.L45R67 2001   j796.962′092   C2001-910748-x

Editing by Lucy Kenward
Cover and text design by Peter Cocking
Front cover photograph by Jim Leary/Bruce Bennett Studios
Back cover photograph by Scott Levy/Bruce Bennett Studios
Printed and bound in Canada by Friesens
Printed on acid-free paper ∞

Every reasonable care has been taken to trace the ownership of copyrighted visual material. Information that will enable the publisher to rectify any reference or credit is welcome.

NHL logos and marks and team logos and marks depicted herein are the property of the NHL and the respective teams and may not be reproduced without the prior written consent of NHL Enterprises, Inc. © 2001 NHL.

We gratefully acknowledge the financial support of the Canada Council for the Arts, the British Columbia Ministry of Tourism, Small Business and Culture, and the Government of Canada through the Book Publishing Industry Development Program for our publishing activities.

Credits

Photography

Photos by Bruce Bennett Studios:
pp. i, 17: Scott Levy · pp. iii, 5, 9, 10, 13, 14, 19, 20, 23, 24, 27, 28, 31, 32, 35, 36, 39, 40, 43, 44, 47, 51, 52: Bruce Bennett · pp. 2, 55: Jim McIsaac

Photos by Allsport:
p. iv: Doug Pensinger · p. 6: Fred Vuich · p. 48: Tom DeFrisco · p. 56: Craig Jones

Photo on page 58 © NHL Images/Dave Sandford

Sources

Canada Cup '87: The Official History. Toronto: No. 1 Productions Ltd., 1987.

Bynum, Mike, ed., *Mario Lemieux: Best There Ever Was*. Toronto: Macmillan Canada, 1997.

Farber, Michael, "League of His Own," *Sports Illustrated*, 12 March 2001, 44–47.

Farber, Michael, "Owner Operator," *Sports Illustrated*, 8 January 2001, 54–58.

Hunter, Douglas. *Scotty Bowman: A Life In Hockey*. Toronto: Penguin Canada, 1998.

Jagr, Jaromir, with Jan Smid. *Jagr: An Autobiography*. Pittsburgh: 68 Productions Ltd., 1997.

Martin, Lawrence, *Mario*. Toronto: Lester Publishing Ltd., 1993.

McMillan, Tom, ed., *Mario Lemieux: The Final Period*. Pittsburgh: Reich, Brisson and Reich Publishing, 1997.

National Hockey League. *National Hockey League Official Guide and Record Book*. Toronto: Dan Diamond and Associates, Inc., 1984–85 to 1997–98.

Paumgarten, Nick, "At the Rink, Puck Naked," *New Yorker*, 19 March 2001, 48.

Tresniowski, Alex, with Cynthia Wang, "Iceman's Return," *People*, 15 January 2001, 58–60.

Hockey Night In Canada on CBC telecast, Toronto Maple Leafs at Pittsburgh Penguins, 27 December, 2000.

Tuesday Night Hockey on CTV SportsNet telecast, Pittsburgh Penguins at Boston Bruins, 9 January, 2001.

A special thank you to Mike Harling, who generously volunteered books and other research materials, game tapes and Internet addresses, without being asked.

01076688

MARIO LEMIEUX

Sean Ross

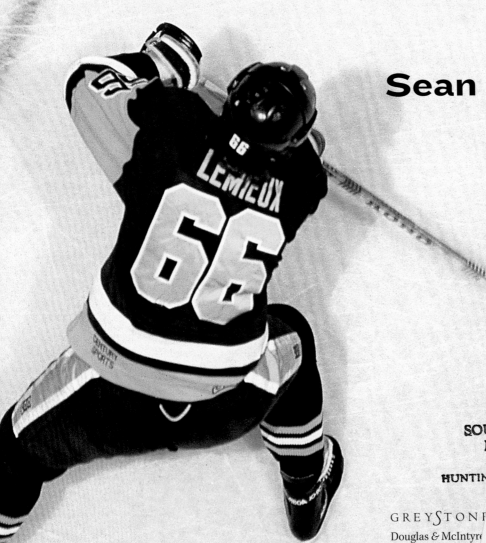

SOUT
PU
2
HUNTIN

GREYSTONE
Douglas & McIntyre
Vancouver/Toronto

M
Re

2. H
I. T
GV8

Editi
Cove
Front
Back
Printe
Printe

Every
copyrig
publish

All NHL
herein a
and may
of NHL E

We grate
Council fo
Small Bus
through th
(BPDIP) fo

CONTENTS

Mario at 35. The kid from Ville Emard comes back in 2000–01, still good for nearly two points per game.

CHAPTER ONE

Beginnings

J UST 30 SECONDS into the first shift of his National Hockey League comeback, Mario Lemieux found himself behind the Toronto Maple Leafs net with the puck on his stick.

Mario passed the puck out in front, where it bounced around on the ice between Leafs defenseman Danny Markov's skates at the right side of the goalmouth. Leafs goalie Curtis Joseph was on his knees, the paddle of his stick flat on the ice, unable to get his glove on the disc. The puck squirted free, toward the open side. Jaromir Jagr, swooping from the goalie's left, jammed it into the net just as a couple more players arrived and banged the net adrift. Red light.

After a short video review, the goal stood. Official time, 33 seconds.

The crowd went wild. But the feeling was less of a celebration than relief. This was the same old Mario, scoring his first point within the first minute of his first shift. Then he followed up with the 614th goal of his career and a further assist in a 5–0 Pittsburgh victory. How many times had Mario done this before?

When he retired in 1997, Mario Lemieux was the most explosive scorer in the NHL. He left the league as its sixth-leading all-time scorer and the only player among the top ten to reach that level in fewer than 1,000 games. His 613 goals in 745 regular-season games translates into the highest goals-per-game average ever recorded—.823—or more than eight goals for each 10 games played. The great Bobby Orr once called Mario the most skilled player he had ever seen. His return was only the latest amazing twist in a remarkable career that began on the outdoor rinks of Ville Emard, Quebec.

PIERRETTE LEMIEUX may be the greatest hockey mom in the history of the game. A story is told in Ville Emard, a working-class suburb of Montreal, that when Pierrette's third son, Mario, was a toddler, he and his older brothers, Alain and Richard, constantly tracked snow into the family's duplex at 6700 rue

Jogues. Alain was four years older, Richard one year. When the snow outside became too deep for the boys to go to the neighborhood rink, Pierrette shovelled snow into the carpeted living room herself, packed it down, and allowed the brothers to play hockey indoors! Maybe it wasn't the best ice, Pierrette noted, but at that time little Mario was skating on his ankles anyway. Pierrette turned down the heat and left the doors open. The carpet, still there nearly 30 years later, stood up quite well.

So did the basement, where the Lemieux boys worked on their stickhandling and shooting skills. Every so often the linoleum floor needed replacing. So did the low tile ceiling, which took a beating when goals were celebrated with uplifted sticks. And so did the piano. With its chipped keys, Pierrette wore Band-Aids to protect her fingers when she played. Even as teenagers the Lemieux boys played in that basement, with cut-down sticks, on their knees.

The winter he turned three, Mario's formal hockey education began. As they had with Alain and Richard before him, Pierrette and her husband Jean-Guy, who built houses for a living, took their youngest son to the nearby Gadbois arena for his first lessons with Fernand Fichaud. It took four or five sessions with Fichaud before little Mario was able to skate without using a chair for support. That was about average. But when the coach saw Mario deke a goalie at age four, he knew that Mario was something special. Fichaud hadn't taught him that move.

On the faceoff Mario eyes the puck. Mark Messier watches a Hall of Famer.

There was never anything average about either Pierrette or Jean-Guy. They are total opposites. Pierrette has been called "a loud and brassy dynamo." Jean-Guy, a man of few words who seldom shows emotion, never missed a Canadiens game at the Montreal Forum. Together, they made hockey the family activity. Long before it became common to do so, both parents attended all of their sons' games and practices. Everything else—school, social life, girls—came a distant second.

"You want to know if there is anything besides hockey that interests me," Mario once said. "The answer is no. At the age of six I separated myself from the others thanks to the way I could handle a stick and puck, and never did the idea of doing anything else other than play hockey ever cross my mind. My life is one long skating rink."

MARIO WAS SIX when his brother's Pee Wee coach invited him to play in an exhibition game with boys who, like Alain, were years older. He scored and had an assist—notable not only because he was so much younger, but also because he was a defenseman at the time. Soon he was playing center and running up as many as six goals a game. Lawrence Martin, author of *Mario,* writes that as an Atom-age player (seven to nine), young Lemieux attracted crowds of three and five thousand to suburban rinks around Montreal.

The eight-year-old Mario had a hard but wild slapshot. Once he accidentally struck an opposing goalie, Carl Parker, in the neck with it. The next time Mario came in on him alone, Parker left the net. Mario tapped in one of the first of his many empty-net goals.

Soon after, Carl and Mario played together on a powerhouse Atom team, the Ville Emard Hurricanes, along with future National Hockey League players J.J. Daigneault, Sylvain Cote, and Marc Bergevin. The same group, calling themselves "The Black Machine," played together from ages seven to 14. Mario, wearing number 27, Alain's number, was by then attracting serious attention, both for the skills that won him the most valuable player (MVP) award at six of the seven tournaments the Hurricanes won with Mario, and for the bad penalties that came from responding to the rough stuff that came with his fame.

During the Quebec Pee Wee championships, his father and his coaches tried to make Mario realize that he was no good to the team in the penalty box. He took penalties, was benched, and was booed by the fans. And Ville Emard was down 6–1 to the Montreal North Pee Wees after two periods. In other words, Mario had his opponents exactly where he wanted them. Mario played the third period. Final score: Mario Lemieux 7, Montreal North 6.

Mario was 13 when Scotty Bowman first saw him play. Montreal Canadiens speedster Yvan "The Roadrunner" Cournoyer saw Mario and told Bowman he was the future of the game. Bowman, then in the midst of coaching the Canadiens to four straight Stanley Cups, came to see Mario play. "I have seen a young man named Mario Lemieux play hockey," is how Bowman was quoted in a French-language newspaper. "He will be a star in the NHL."

Mario poses with his parents,

Jean-Guy and Pierrette, and

wife-to-be, Nathalie (in pink).

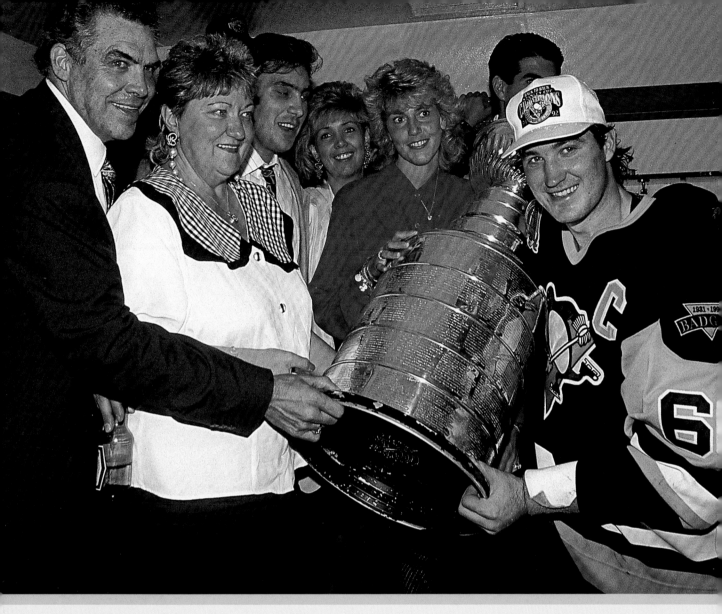

Family Ties

"I've had a strong sense of family since I was very young," Mario Lemieux says in his autobiography, *The Final Period,* "because my parents instilled it in me. In our little Montreal suburb of Ville Emard, we probably had ten families of relatives within two blocks, and we were always together. Brothers, cousins, uncles. It seemed like you could go to any street in the community and find one of our relatives...."

And his wife? "Nathalie Asselin was 15 years old when I met her through—what else?—a family connection. My cousin is married to her cousin, and that's how we got together... I guess you could say the rest is history."

Mario's parents still live in the duplex in which he grew up; he has offered to buy a "newer, bigger house in another part of town. I'm still offering. But my mother's got her sister and her entire extended family there, and she's used to the same things all the time, the same routine."

Mario, 18, all-time

Quebec League

scoring champ, takes

in his new home,

Pittsburgh.

CHAPTER TWO

Promises, Promises

"I JUST FELL in love with him. I saw great things for him the first day I saw him," remembers Bob Perno, a player agent in Quebec. A couple of years after reading Scotty Bowman's prediction of National Hockey League stardom for Mario, "I went to a hockey school in the summer at McGill University," Perno told a Pittsburgh writer. "I looked down on the ice and I saw this big kid out there skating through everybody. I asked, 'Who is that guy?'" It was Mario. "That night, I called Gus [Badali, Wayne Gretzky's agent and an associate of Perno's] and said, 'This guy is good. This guy is another Wayne.'"

Perno met the Lemieux family at home. At 15, Mario had finished a year of Midget AAA hockey, scoring 62 goals in 40 games. Lawrence Martin sets the scene in *Mario:* there he was, sitting in front of his parents, saying that he could break the Quebec Major Junior Hockey League (QMJHL) scoring records and become the top junior player in the world. This was before he had played a single game of junior hockey. If he did that, he asked Perno, "How big a contract do you think you can get me?"

"Well," Perno said, "it's hard to say. But if you break the records and are the first pick in the NHL draft, I think you will become a millionaire with your first contract."

"A million dollars!" Mario exclaimed. "I'll get a million dollars? You're sure?"

"Yes," Perno promised. "I'll get you a million."

Mario shook Perno's hand and said, "You are my agent." Their contract was a handshake.

MARIO WAS CHOSEN first in the 1981 QMJHL draft that summer, joining the last-place Laval Voisins. Mario promised owner Claude Fournel a Memorial Cup, Canadian junior hockey's championship trophy.

In Mario's first season of junior hockey, 1981–82, he scored 96 points, the highest total of any first-year QMJHL player, and he drew crowds of 4,000 to the Centre Sportif Laval. But Sylvain Turgeon was named QMJHL Rookie of the Year.

Disappointed, Mario decided to quit school after Grade 10 to concentrate on hockey. Perno and Badali tried to change his mind, and even Gretzky urged Mario to stay in school, all to no avail. "In a sense," Mario has explained, "that's when I became a pro."

The following year found Mario in a race for the league scoring lead with St. Louis native Pat LaFontaine. The American was fast on the ice and a quick wit off it, and reporters covering the Quebec League loved him. Mario felt overshadowed on his home turf.

To prove himself, Mario was playing 40 minutes a game, a load that may have caused his back problems to appear for the first time.

During the 1982 Christmas break, Mario was invited to play on Canada's team in the World Junior

The Mario Lemieux File

Position: Center, Left wing

Born: October 5, 1965, Montreal, Quebec

Height: Six feet four inches (1.93 meters)

Weight: 234 pounds (106 kilograms)

Shoots: Right

Number: 66

Nickname: Super Mario, Le Magnifique

Hobbies: Nintendo, wine cellar

Off-season sports: Golf

Childhood Hockey Hero: Guy Lafleur

Hockey Highlight: Winning first Stanley Cup in 1991

Championships, held in the former Russian capital of Leningrad. Everything went wrong. Coach Dave King put him on the fourth line, Mario missed three games, and the Canadians lost to the gold medal-winning Soviets 7–3, returning home with bronze medals. Back in Quebec, LaFontaine had added to his 30-point lead over Mario in the scoring race. Mario's play declined during the second half of the season, partly due to his back spasms. Laval finished first in the QMJHL, but was bounced from the playoffs.

Mario told Perno that, if invited to the World Juniors in 1983, he would not go. The issue of whether Mario could be forced to go ended up in court. Having signed a contract with one of its member clubs, the QMJHL argued, the 17-year-old could be ordered to play international hockey. The court did not agree. Mario won, but defending his right not to play for his country damaged his reputation.

IN HIS FINAL YEAR of junior hockey, 1983–84, Mario's game continued to improve—largely because he could finally see. He began wearing contact lenses. That year Laval won 54 of 70 regular-season games. Mario had a 61-game scoring streak. And he broke two longstanding records: the QMJHL marks for scoring and total points.

Mario passed Pierre Larouche's 251 points with five games remaining in the season. But, with four games left, he was still 12 goals behind his boyhood hero Guy Lafleur's 130. He netted four against Chicoutimi but only one versus Shawinigan. In the final two games he needed seven goals. He got four in the first game against Quebec.

Going into the last game, against the Longueuil Chevaliers, he raised the stakes by inviting Gretzky and Paul Coffey, in town to play with the Oilers the following night, to watch. Pittsburgh Penguins general manager Ed Johnston was there too. But Mario knew that the more pressure he faced, the better he would play.

That game is now legend. Mario scored at 43 seconds, then again at 2:03. He tied Lafleur's mark of 130 goals at 1:18 of the second period. Then, at seven minutes, he tipped in another goal off the faceoff. The arena erupted, Mario was mobbed by his teammates, and the QMJHL goal-scoring record was his, just as he had foreseen at the age of 15.

Mario shoots on North Star goalie Jon Casey during the 1991 Stanley Cup Final.

Mario scored twice more, for a total of six goals in the game and 133 for the season. Twice he passed to teammates for easy empty-net scores, giving him five assists, a total of 11 points for the night, and an unbelievable 282 for the season.

After the game, Mario reminded Perno of that night at the Lemieux household three years before. "Remember you told me how much I would get if I broke the records?

"Well," he said, "I've done my job."

Well, not quite. There was still the Memorial Cup. In 14 Quebec League playoff games, Mario scored no less than 52 points—another league record. Laval swept their series with Drummondville and Granby, and beat Longueuil in six games for the 1984 provincial title. But at the Memorial Cup tournament in Kitchener, the Voisins were outplayed by bigger, more physical Ontario and Western teams. Mario scored four goals during the tournament, but they were not enough; Laval went home without the Cup.

Having delivered on his side of the bargain with Bob Perno, Mario fully expected a million-dollar contract. No rookie had come close to that amount up to then. Then too, no rookie had come into the NHL with numbers like his.

The Pittsburgh Penguins were eager to sign him. GM Ed Johnston had traded away the Penguins' best defenseman and demoted their best goalie to the minors. The club finished last in the NHL with the worst record in franchise history. So hungry were the Penguins for Mario that they made him a generous offer—$700,000 over three seasons—even before the draft took place. But Mario wanted the million. Both sides dug in their heels.

The night before the Entry Draft, which was due to take place at the Montreal Forum on June 9, 1984, Pittsburgh made its final offer: $760,000. Mario said it was a million or nothing. He would play golf on draft day; he wouldn't even show up at the Forum.

Perno was appalled. Badali and Perno called Wayne Gretzky. Contract or no, Gretzky advised, Mario should show up. He could refuse to put on his new team's sweater, but he had to be there. Mario cancelled his golf game.

Having finished last in the league, Pittsburgh selected first in the Entry Draft. When, as expected, the Penguins announced the name Mario Lemieux, "Numero soixante-six," the NHL's first draft pick for 1984 stayed seated in the stands. Johnston repeated his name. A Pittsburgh scout, who was an old friend of the family, climbed the steps to the Lemieux seats and ordered Mario to come down and don the sweater. An argument ensued.

As the Lemieux family left the Forum, Mario told reporters, "I'm not going to put on the sweater if they don't want me bad enough." The press accused him of being a prima donna. What should have been the happiest day of his life so far became, for Mario, a disaster. A year before, hockey fans had seen him refuse to play for his country. Now he looked not only stubborn but greedy.

Penguins' Early Bird

Mario Lemieux's trademark is to light up the
scoreboard early and often in big games. Here's
a brief selection:

Last regular-season junior game: Mario scores
at 43 seconds and 2:03 of the first period, then at
1:18 of the second to tie Guy Lafleur's 1970–71
Quebec League record of 130 goals. Game totals:
six goals, five assists.

First NHL shift: Scores on a breakaway at 2:59.

1989 playoffs vs Philadelphia: Mario scores on a
breakaway at 2:15; has a hat trick in 4:40. Game
totals: five goals and eight points to break a 2–2
series deadlock.

1990 NHL All-Star game: Mario scores the first-ever
All-Star first period hat trick, the first of those goals
at 21 seconds. Game total: four goals.

First comeback game: Mario sets up Jagr and earns
his 1,495th NHL point at 33 seconds.

Mario made a lasting

impression on the

first shift of his first

NHL game. He has

never looked back.

CHAPTER THREE

Making the NHL

YEARS LATER, Mario would admit that he had made a mistake. The Lemieux family knew it right away. A compromise was reached on Mario's first contract when the family drove to Perno's house the Sunday after the Entry Draft and decided to accept a contract for the money Pittsburgh was offering, which included a $100,000 signing bonus plus bonuses that might make him a millionaire if he quickly became a top scorer in the National Hockey League.

And he did. Mario scored on his first shift in the NHL—against, of all defensemen, Boston Bruins All-Star Ray Bourque. Bourque's pass up-ice struck one of Mario's skates, giving him a breakaway on goalie Pete Peeters.

Six days later, Pittsburgh's home opener against the Vancouver Canucks drew nearly 14,741 fans—nearly 10,000 more than a game with the Canucks normally attracted. At 18 seconds, Mario set up the first goal in a 4–3 win.

Still, "the first 10 games were really tough," Mario reflected later, "because I felt a lot of pressure on me to do well and maybe I was trying too hard. I guess I ran into all the things that players do when they come in from junior hockey. The pace is faster, the players are bigger, stronger, and smarter, and if you make a mistake, they take advantage of it.

"At first I felt that the things I had done in junior hockey just wouldn't work in the NHL, and that limited me a lot. Then I started to realize that they would work, but that I just had to do them that much faster and not hold onto the puck so long." Pittsburgh coach Bob Berry worked with him on aspects of the game that had not seemed so important in junior: faceoffs and checking.

Mario continued his rookie year at a better than point-a-game pace, which got him named to the NHL All-Star game by Prince of Wales Conference coach Al Arbour. (From 1974–75 to 1993–94, the NHL was divided into two conferences: the Prince of Wales and the Clarence Campbell Conference.)

Before the All-Star game, former Bruins coach and TV commentator Don Cherry called Mario "the biggest floater in the game." Mario reacted to the criticism as he always does: he scored twice and set up another goal to take All-Star MVP honors in a 6–4 Wales Conference win.

Pittsburgh's general manager Ed Johnston thought the All-Star game was a turning point for Mario. Winning the MVP award "really made him feel he belonged. From then on he took off." Mario's 100 points were the third-best output by a rookie in NHL history. He was 19 years old. Pittsburgh was consistently drawing 3,000 more fans per game than they had the previous season.

Perno's million-dollar promise was fulfilled that summer. Pittsburgh rewrote Mario's contract to pay him $500,000 a year. This would be the last

Pick a Number

Fifteen-year-old Mario Lemieux and his agent, Bob Perno, were aboard a train en route to Wayne Gretzky's annual celebrity golf tournament in Brantford, when Perno brought up the question of what number a future superstar should wear. Mario was happy wearing number 27, his older brother Alain's number, but Perno insisted that all-time greats should have their own numbers.

"Okay, Mario says, I'll take 99."

Perno doesn't think so: "There's only one Wayne Gretzky and there's only one Mario Lemieux," he says.

"So what should I do?" Mario asks.

"Why not 66?" Perno suggests.

contract Perno obtained for Mario. The Pittsburgh family he lived with during his rookie year, the Mathews, knew a more powerful agent, Tom Reich.

THE 1985 WORLD CHAMPIONSHIPS held in Prague, Czechoslovakia, were moved from their normal time in April, when the NHL playoffs are underway, to summer, giving players on the NHL's best teams a chance to play. Mario was invited, but, as usual, not excited. He was the only French-speaking player on the team. He sat out two games with a groin injury, including a 9–1 loss to the Soviet Union. He demanded to be sent home. But when he watched the Canadians lose to the United States, Mario saw what a difference he could make to the team. He changed his mind about leaving.

With Mario playing, Canada beat Finland to make the semifinals, where they met the mighty Soviets, the gold-medal winners at the 1984 Sarajevo Winter Olympics. Canada had not beaten them since 1961. Jaromir Jagr remembers watching the game on television as a 13 year old. "Lemieux enchanted the people of Prague. From the moment I laid eyes on him, he became my hockey hero. It never occurred to me that one day I'd be playing with him on the same team."

Lemieux scored two of Canada's goals against the Soviets in a 3–1 victory. And he became a hero to the people of Prague by helping to defeat the Soviets, a rare event that always went over well in Czechoslovakia. Then the Czechs beat Canada in the final, 5–3, in a game that could have gone either way.

Winning the silver medal changed Mario's attitude toward international hockey, "Doing this is a greater thrill than I ever dreamed of," he said to amazed reporters. "Of course I would come here again."

AFTER THREE SEASONS in the National Hockey League, scoring 100 points or more in each, Mario Lemieux was a work in progress. In 1985–86, his second season, he played 79 regular-season games, more than he ever would again, and amassed 141 points, second to Wayne Gretzky's 215. Despite missing 17 games, he was the NHL's third-leading scorer in 1986–87 with 107 points, one point behind Jari Kurri, Gretzky's (183 points) right wing.

The Penguins had not made the playoffs since Lemieux's arrival, partly because they played in the tough Patrick Division, which was dominated by the second-best team in the league, the Philadelphia Flyers. The Penguins had finished fifth or lower each of the previous five years, but there was a positive side to all of this losing. Beginning with Mario in 1984, the Penguins never picked worse than fifth in the first round of the Entry Draft for five consecutive seasons.

Mario, the third-highest scoring rookie in NHL history, with his 1984 Calder Trophy.

And the Penguins *were* improving. With Lemieux, the club had climbed from the 50-point level to more than 70 points in each of the past two seasons. But many people thought that Pittsburgh could do better if Mario would only bear down harder. Sportswriter Dave Molinari, then of the Pittsburgh *Press,* wrote, "If he ever decides to show up for work 80 nights a year, Lemieux could be the best—yes, the best—player in the NHL. If not, he will always be a pale copy of Wayne Gretzky, and the Penguins will remain mired in mediocrity."

A Mario Lemieux needs to do more than rack up eye-popping statistics and make his team better. The best players compete in the global arena. Mario's record there was mixed. Despite the big impression he left with the 13-year-old Jaromir Jagr, Mario had not yet shown himself and the hockey world what he could do against the very best players anywhere.

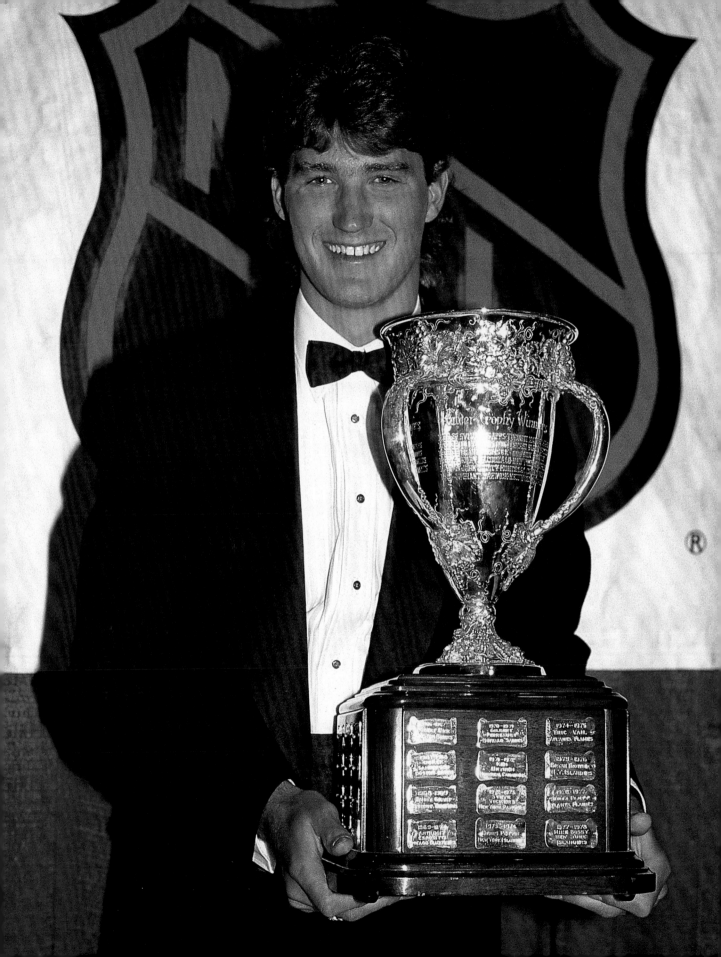

Mario has often been compared with Wayne Gretzky. Playing together, they made hockcy history during the 1987 Canada Cup tournament.

CHAPTER FOUR

Fifteen Days in September

N INETEEN EIGHTY-SEVEN was a feast of international hockey. That year the National Hockey League All-Star game was junked in favor of a two-game series between the Soviet national team and the NHL All-Stars, held in Quebec City and called Rendez-Vous 87. And there would be a third Canada Cup tournament.

Matchups between the Soviets and NHL players were always exciting: in 55 outings against NHL clubs, the Soviets had won 35 games, lost 18, and tied twice. In the first NHL-Soviet All-Star game, February 11, Mario assisted on two goals, including the winner, in a 4–3 NHL win. The Soviets won the second game two nights later, 5–3, with Mario assisting on the NHL's third goal with 37 seconds left in the game.

With the Penguins finishing out of the playoffs again, Mario was invited to join Canada's team of players from non-playoff clubs at the World Championships in Vienna, Austria. Pressure to go came from all sides: from Alan Eagleson, the players' association head and international hockey organizer, and from players such as Marcel Dionne, who said of Mario, "I think he can push himself a little bit harder." Competing for your country, Dionne added, is one of "the things great players do. That's how you gain respect from your peers." Mario said no thanks.

As always, when Mario made up his mind, nothing could move him. Canada fought to a scoreless draw with the Soviets, then lost for the first time ever to West Germany, before falling to eventual champions Sweden, 9–0. Some said Mario should not be invited to play in the fourth Canada Cup.

But he was. And he was keen to play.

Canada Cup 87 has been called the finest exhibition of hockey ever seen. Only the top hockey nations were invited: Sweden, the Soviet Union, Czechoslovakia, Finland, the U.S., and, of course, Canada. A great generation of players was on the rise or at their peak. Wayne Gretzky's NHL-record 215-point season was little more than a year in the past. The Soviet Union's famous KLM Line— Vladimir Krutov, Igor Larionov, and Sergei Makarov—was in its glory. Makarov would be the tournament's third-leading scorer, behind Gretzky and Lemieux. Czechoslovakia's Dominik Hasek was not yet "The Dominator," but he showed signs of greatness.

Mario and a Soviet player

look for the puck during the

1987 Canada Cup.

Mario appeared at Team Canada's August training camp in Montreal, where he seemed bored until the games got underway. Then, in a pre-tournament exhibition game against the Soviets, he pumped in four goals. In a round-robin game against the U.S., egged on by a heckler in Hamilton, Mario scored all three goals in a 3–1 win for Canada. Then he notched two goals and an assist against the world champions, Sweden.

Canada faced off against Czechoslovakia for the right to meet the Soviets in the three-game final. The Czechs did all the scoring in the first period, going ahead 2–0. Again, Mario rose to the occasion with two goals and an assist. Sent in alone on Hasek, Mario flipped the puck in off the goalie and the far post to tie the game 2–2. One minute and 43 seconds later, on a power play, Mario redirected a

cross-ice pass from Ray Bourque into the open side of the net for the go-ahead goal. When the Czechs replied to come within one, Mario set up Brian Propp for the insurance goal. As sensational as Mario was, the best was yet to come.

Game One, Canada vs. Soviet Union, Montreal, September 11:
Mario assisted on Canada's first two goals, which came before and after a four-goal Soviet outburst. Despite having a goal disallowed, Canada overcame a three-goal deficit to tie the game and appeared to have won it when Gretzky scored with 2:59 left. But the Soviets scored 32 seconds later to tie, and then won 5:33 into overtime. USSR 6, Canada 5.

Game Two, Hamilton, September 13, "the greatest hockey game ever played":
Midway through the second period, the Soviets had overcome a two-goal Canadian lead to tie at 3–3. Canadian coach Mike Keenan, who used 17 line combinations during the game, put Gretzky and Lemieux together for the first time. From then on, the two ruled. Two minutes after the tying goal, Gretzky passed to Lemieux to go ahead.

The Soviets tied the game at 4–4, and the Canadians wilted. For two minutes the crowd chanted "Go Canada Go." Gretzky found Lemieux at the far side of the Soviet net, and Canada led 5–4. But, with 64 seconds left in the game, Valeri Kamensky split the Canadian defense and roofed the puck as he fell backward.

The game went into overtime, and although the Soviets outshot Canada 12–9, neither team scored. The second overtime started slowly until Brian Propp's pass from behind the Soviet net to incoming defenseman Larry Murphy

Mario Lemieux vs Wayne Gretzky

Wayne Gretzky has far and away the best career scoring totals; he holds or shares 61 records: 40 regular season, 15 playoff, and six All-Star game. Mario Lemieux is second in at least 19 instances.

Yet Mario's goal-per-game average (.823) is the highest ever recorded. In any game, Mario was more likely to score than any NHL player ever. Gretzky agreed: playing on a line with Mario in the 1987 Canada Cup, he made Mario the trigger-man.

Former Montreal goalie Ken Dryden has said of Mario: "To me, he's the only person in the league who can embarrass you. The others can beat you. He embarrasses you."

turned the game. Murphy got the puck to Gretzky at the left side of the net. Gretzky shot, Evgeny Belosheikin made the save, and Lemieux, at the other side of the net, shovelled in the rebound. Canada 6, USSR 5.

Game Three, Hamilton, September 15:

"The whole game was like sudden death," said Soviet assistant coach Igor Dimitriev. It started after a 12-minute standing ovation for both teams, but the racket ended at 26 seconds when Krutov, behind the Canadian net, fed Makarov, who scored. After eight minutes, the Soviets had scored two more unlikely goals, one off both posts, the other when stay-at-home defenseman Viacheslav Fetisov walked in alone on Canadian goalie Grant Fuhr.

Two minutes later, Rick Tocchet, playing hurt, banged a rebound past Sergei Mylnikov. Six minutes after that, Tocchet fed the puck to Brian Propp, who put it in. USSR 3, Canada 2. With 26 seconds left in the first period, the Soviets scored again, making it 4–2.

The game got physical in the second period. Vyacheslav Bykov tripped Mario at 8:24, and on the power play Mario fed Gretzky behind the Soviet net; Gretzky found Murphy coming from the point, and Murphy buried the puck. Canada followed with two more goals to go ahead 5–4. The USSR tied it at 12:21 of the third period.

With one minute and 36 seconds left on the clock, Dale Hawerchuk won the faceoff, Mario took the puck, passed up-ice to Gretzky, and lit the afterburners himself, following the play. As Gretzky, Murphy, and then Mario crossed the Soviet blueline, coach Dimitriev thought to himself, "It is finished."

Mario's top-shelf goal, on a back pass by Gretzky, may be the most replayed score in hockey history. It was Mario's Canada Cup–leading 11th goal—four ahead of the USSR's Makarov and Krutov—and it left him second in total points with 18 to Gretzky's 21. Gretzky was named the tournament's MVP.

AFTER THE SOVIET overtime victory in the first game of the final, Gretzky said, "I have been under a lot of pressure for a long time. I would like nothing better than to have someone else win the NHL scoring title. And it's just a matter of time before Mario takes over."

Maybe less time than he thought.

Goalies Salute Mario

How does a great scorer do it? Ask the goalie he practices against. Gilles Meloche joined the Penguins in 1985 and played three seasons with Mario Lemieux. On the deke, Mario's reach, extended by his 63-inch stick, is the decisive weapon.

"He comes across the crease and you aren't going to give him time to bury you," Meloche explains. "So you reach and he pulls the puck back a little farther, and then you can't reach anymore and he still has something left.

"When I'm watching from the other end of the ice, it seems like Mario, with that stride of his, is almost in the corner by now and I'm saying to myself 'Shoot it Mario, dammit, shoot it.'"

Kelly Hrudy remembers Mario's one-timer shot. "He had the hardest shot off the wing of anybody on one-timers," Hrudy recalled between periods of Mario's comeback game against Toronto, as tape was shown of Mario beating him high on the glove side. "I don't feel bad. He won the Canada Cup on a shot like that."

The face of a

champion. Mario in

1990–91, when the

years of team building

were finally rewarded

with the Stanley Cup.

CHAPTER FIVE

Climbing the Mountain

"THE 87 CANADA CUP changed Mario Lemieux," says Craig Simpson, now a hockey broadcaster, who played most of three seasons with Mario. "It changed his attitude. It changed his focus."

In 1987–88 new Pittsburgh coach Pierre Creamer put Mario on the penalty-killing unit and at the point on the power play. Counting his regular shift on the Penguins' top line, Mario was soon playing half of each game. With all the ice time, he began the season by scoring 28 points in the first 14 games. Yet the Penguins won only one of their first eight games.

In late November, Ed Johnston traded four players to Edmonton for Paul Coffey, the outstanding offensive defenseman of his time. Just like that, Coffey's crisp outlet passes were going to Mario instead of Wayne Gretzky. Pittsburgh went 8–3–1 in the team's next dozen games. Mario increased his points total to 67 in his first 30 games. In December, Gretzky was injured, and Mario took over the lead in the scoring race.

The 1988 All-Star game served further notice that Mario had found a new level of play. His six points set a new All-Star game record, and he was voted All-Star MVP—best of the best—for a second time in his four years in the league.

He kept up the pace in the second half of the season. In a six-game stretch starting in mid-March, he earned 20 points. Mario won his first National Hockey League scoring title, with 168 points. The club won eight of its last 11 games, finishing 36–35–9 for its first winning season in nine years. But Pittsburgh missed the playoffs again, this time by two points.

Mario won the Hart Trophy as the league's MVP, the Lester B. Pearson Award as the league's MVP voted by the players, and the Art Ross Trophy as the NHL's leading scorer, saying at the NHL awards dinner, "I thought it was about time this year that I started to show my stuff. It started at the Canada Cup, playing with Wayne…."

THE PENGUINS' OWNER was not happy with the team's progress. He replaced Johnston with former Blackhawks goaltending star Tony Esposito, and Creamer with Gene Ubriaco, an original Penguin and a veteran minor-league coach.

In 1988–89 the Penguins continued to improve, winning 40 games, which was a franchise record. A key addition was former Buffalo goaltender Tom Barrasso.

Mario had three eight-point games that season: against St. Louis on October 15, against New Jersey on New Year's Eve 1988, and again on April 25, 1989, in the playoffs against Philadelphia. He set a Pittsburgh club record with the eight points against St. Louis. But the New Jersey game stands out because five of his eight points were goals, and they were scored in all five possible ways: five-on-five, shorthanded, power play, penalty shot, and empty net. Among those points was his 100th of the season, scored third-fastest in NHL history. Mario's big night earned Pittsburgh an 8–6 victory and moved the Penguins into first place in their division, unseating the Devils.

The first-ever three-time

NHL All-Star Game

MVP signs autographs.

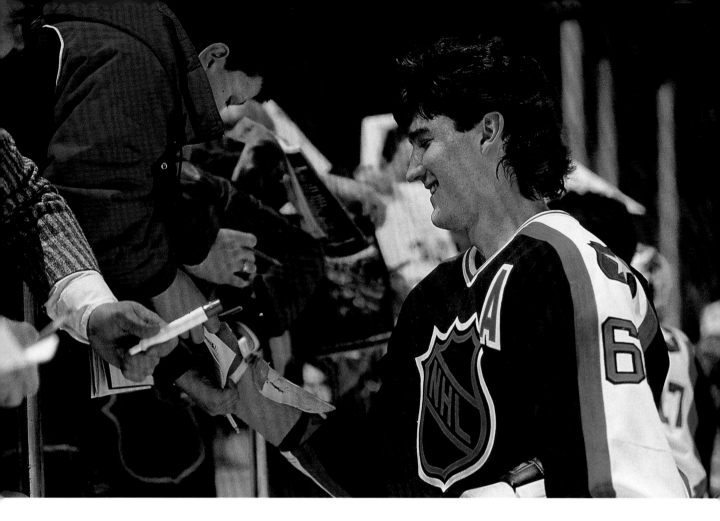

In the playoffs for the first time in seven years, Pittsburgh swept the New York Rangers in their division semifinal, but lost a see-saw seven-game final to Philadelphia despite Mario's eight-point game. Mario scored at 2:15 and had a natural hat trick (three consecutive goals) by 4:40 of the first period, leading the Penguins to a 10–7 win and a 3–2 series lead. But the Flyers won the next two games to eliminate Pittsburgh.

Once again Mario led the NHL in scoring with 85 goals and 199 points, and once again he won the Hart, Pearson, and Ross trophies. With Wayne Gretzky traded to the Los Angeles Kings, a team that was weaker than the Edmonton team he had led to four Stanley Cups, he was less of a threat in the scoring race. Mario and the Penguins were finally on the edge of success.

"We knew we didn't have the team to win the Cup that year," Mario later recalled. "But it was a good experience for the organization just to get back in the playoffs and see what it took. We definitely built on that."

But 1988–89 was also Mario Lemieux's last pain-free season. He would become more of a hockey hero than ever, but not in a way he wanted.

The Penguins began to look like a Stanley Cup-winning club in 1989–90 when Craig Patrick took over as general manager of the team. Patrick came from two generations of Hockey Hall-of-Famers. He took over the coaching midway through a disappointing season, 32–40–8, which left Pittsburgh fifth in the Patrick Division, and once again out of the playoffs. Patrick hired Scotty Bowman, winner of five Stanley Cups with Montreal, as Director of Player Development and Recruitment. Almost immediately Bowman signed Mark Recchi, who scored 30 goals in his first full season with Pittsburgh.

After winning three straight, the Penguins went into a four-game tailspin, including an 8–4 loss to Los Angeles on October 31. Starting with that game, Mario scored a point or more in the 18 games leading up to the All-Star break on January 21, 1990.

Pittsburgh hosted the 1990 classic, which was the first NHL All-Star game to be aired on U.S. network television since 1960. Mario scored on his first three shots to record the first-ever first-period hat trick and the second-ever four-goal All-Star game. Of course he was named the MVP, the first player ever to be All-Star MVP three times.

Mario continued his points streak into February. But the back pain that had come and gone since his junior days was there to stay. He tried to play through the pain. Unable to tie his skates or shoes, Mario, by his own estimate, became half the player he had been—although he still managed to extend his points streak for another couple of weeks.

Mario stops on a dime

and dangles the puck as

the defense backs off.

On February 14, Mario played his regular shift through the first period at Madison Square Garden, then told coach Patrick, "I can't help the team." He cut back to one shift and two power plays in the second, but could not appear for the third period. Mario's consecutive-game point streak ended at 46 games—still the second-longest such streak after Gretzky's record of 51. He scored 39 goals and 103 points in those 46 games, and was leading the league in scoring with 121 points at the time.

He missed the next 21 games, spending six weeks in Los Angeles trying a special program to improve his back without an operation. He did feel better.

With the playoffs in the balance, Mario played 25 minutes in the season finale against Buffalo, including a four-minute stretch, scoring a goal and an assist. Pittsburgh lost in overtime, missing the playoffs by one point.

ON JUNE 16, 1990, in Vancouver, Pittsburgh picked Jaromir Jagr first in the Entry Draft. The same day, the club acquired Joe Mullen, who had notched 51 goals a year before. And Patrick signed Bob Johnson, former Calgary Flames and U.S. national team coach, to replace himself as coach. Patrick would add Bryan Trottier, winner of four Stanley Cups with the Islanders, in July.

A few days after the draft, Jagr visited Pittsburgh. Patrick invited Czechs living in the Steel City to a party where Jagr could choose a family to live with for the upcoming season. As Jagr remembers it:

"There was a sudden commotion with the arrival of one unexpected guest. Mario Lemieux. I was pleasantly surprised when I saw Mario and his then-fiancée, Nathalie, but the people who knew better were beside themselves. What was he doing at a little party to welcome some 18-year-old kid from Czechoslovakia?

"And then something happened that I will never forget. Mario came up to me, extended his hand and said, 'If you need anything, you can always come to me. I was in the exact same situation as you are now when I came to Pittsburgh speaking only French, and I still remember how hard it was. So don't worry, I know the problems you'll be having, and I know how you're feeling. I'm ready to help you at any time.'"

THAT JULY 11 Mario had back surgery. The operation was a success but the doctor found a crack in the bone that might cause trouble in the future. In mid-September, Mario awoke in pain. "I couldn't even stand up," he has said.

The diagnosis was a disk-space infection, which the doctor said could threaten Mario's career. With the right medication, he thought, Mario might be back on skates in three months. He had missed 31 games of the last season, played one game, and now the doctors were saying he would be lucky to play half the upcoming 1990–91 season.

At that moment, with Pittsburgh's NHL season starting without him, Mario could never have imagined what the next eight months would bring.

Comeback King

Mario's Lemieux's comeback three-and-a-half years after retiring from the National Hockey League was only his latest in a series of returns from prolonged absence. Each layoff triggered a scoring spree within 10 games.

Comeback Year	Games Missed	Reason	Points in First 10 games
1990–91	54	back surgery	7 goals, 21 points
1992–93	24	back problems, Hodgkin's disease	14 goals, 26 points
1995–96	62 in 1993–94, entire 1994–95 season	recovering from cancer treatments	13 goals, 32 points

The highlight of

Mario's hockey career

was lifting the Stanley

Cup for the first

time. He was voted

playoff MVP.

CHAPTER SIX

The Stanley Cup

"I SEE THE GAME a lot differently now," Mario said after missing the first half of the 1990–91 season. "Every time I have a chance to play the game I think I'll approach it a lot differently. It makes you think a lot and realize how lucky you are."

The antibiotics the doctors gave Mario worked. His back infection cleared up, and Mario skated again at the end of December. He was eager to play, not only because he missed hockey, but because he could see the team getting better. Penguins hockey was becoming fun to play.

Bob Johnson, nicknamed "Badger Bob" for the 15 seasons he coached the University of Wisconsin Badgers, was the tonic the Penguins needed. "I definitely enjoyed playing for Badger," Mario said later. "He was the best for picking up your confidence. Every day it was 'You guys are the best, you guys are great players.' He never said anything negative."

And it was true that, more and more, the Penguins were becoming a fine team. Gordie Roberts brought playoff experience with him from St. Louis. Defenseman Larry Murphy joined Coffey in giving Pittsburgh two great power-play quarterbacks. Jiri Hrdina added depth at center and became a Czech-speaking friend for Jaromir Jagr, who pulled out of a 15-game scoring slump one week after Hrdina joined the team.

January 26, 1991, was Mario's first day of the season. He had three assists in a 6–5 win over the Quebec Nordiques, but the team struggled through February. So, in early March, Patrick traded for big defenseman Ulf Samuelsson and center Ron Francis, hoping to boost his team's chances in the playoffs. The Penguins' chances only got better when Mario scored two power-play goals and one shorthanded in a 3–1 win over Philadelphia, taking Pittsburgh to within a point of the Patrick Division championship and the playoff home-ice advantage.

For Jagr, the playoffs showed a side of Mario that he had never seen before. It was as if the reserved, even-tempered superstar "becomes someone else. He gets into conversations and starts psyching up the rest of the team.... And as the ultimate goal got closer and closer, Mario grew zealous, rousing every team-mate and hammering it into our heads that we were going to do it."

In the first round, New Jersey, another rising team, took the Penguins to seven games. Then Pittsburgh eked out come-from-behind victories over Washington and Boston to play for the Stanley Cup.

Stanley Cup Milestone

Just over 15 minutes into the second period of the 1991 Stanley Cup final, the Penguins led the second game against Minnesota 2–1, but Minnesota was pressing for the equalizer.

Mario Lemieux took a lead pass from Phil Bourque and crossed the North Star blueline. Defensemen Shawn Chambers and Neil Wilkinson backpedaled about 12 feet inside their zone. Mario faked to the middle, then moved the puck to his backhand side, as if to go around Chambers. As Chambers committed to the outside, Mario split the two defensemen. In on Minnesota goalie Jon Casey, Mario shifted right, to his forehand, then crossed to his backhand, putting the puck into the left corner. Pittsburgh 3, Minnesota 1. Biographer Lawrence Martin called it "one of the most exquisite goals of Stanley Cup history."

IN THE FINAL, Pittsburgh met Minnesota. The North Stars had finished the season far under .500 and 20 points behind the Penguins, but had ridden the goaltending of Jon Casey to the big dance.

Once again, Pittsburgh lost the first game. Even though the Penguins were leading 2–1 at the midway point in Game Two, Mario remembers, "They played better than us the first half of the game, and ... I thought we were in a lot of trouble." So he took the game into his own hands.

Phil Bourque passed up-ice to Mario in the neutral zone. With a series of fakes to the outside, he got Minnesota defenseman Shawn Chambers to commit that way, then split Chambers and his partner, Neil Wilkinson. In alone on Casey, he deked right, to his forehand, and tapped the puck inside the left post, backhand, as he fell.

In its style and timing, Mario's solo dash was the killing blow. Sportswriter Dave Molinari wrote that "Lemieux stole whatever jump the North Stars had when he scored his spectacular goal. The one that kept the Penguins in this series. The one that might have made a Stanley Cup possible." Pittsburgh took the game, 4–1.

Minnesota won the third game when Mario was unable to play because of back spasms. In Game Four, Kevin Stevens, Francis, and Mario scored in the first three minutes and then held on behind Tom Barrasso's goaltending to take a stranglehold on the series. In the fifth game the Penguins repeated the formula; Game Six was a blowout, 8–0.

Mario and Kevin Stevens celebrate during the 1991–92 Stanley Cup final.

Mario won the Conn Smythe Trophy as the Stanley Cup MVP with a playoff-leading 16 goals and 44 points in 23 games, but he was upset to lose the Hart Trophy to Brett Hull.

More devastating was Bob Johnson's collapse on August 26, two days before the opening of the 1991 Canada Cup. The coach had two cancer tumors in his brain, only one of which could be removed. Team USA, playing for Badger Bob, made the tournament final against Canada. Mario, still nursing his back, did not play.

SCOTTY BOWMAN replaced Badger Bob as Pittsburgh's coach for 1991–92, a move that was delayed out of respect for Johnson until after training camp. Johnson died November 26, at age 61. "While Bowman might have been the new coach," writes Doug Hunter, Scotty Bowman's biographer, "the team was still playing for the old one." Bowman, the opposite in personal style to Johnson, left the everyday coaching to his assistants, Barry Smith and long-time Penguin Rick Kehoe.

Seldom has a Stanley Cup-champion team looked less like repeating than Pittsburgh did. Three big guns—Stevens, Recchi, and Francis—went into training camp unsigned. The team was sold. Pittsburgh was inconsistent, winning and losing by large margins. January 26, 1992, Mario was mugged by Washington, fought back, complained to the referee, was ejected from the game and assessed a 10-game suspension and $1,000 fine for running into the official. He complained about the clutch-and-grab style of hockey that was becoming more common, and called the NHL "a garage league." He talked about retiring at age 26. He blasted another referee on February 15. Then his back went into spasm again.

That month Coffey was traded for two players and a draft choice, and Recchi was exchanged for defenseman Kjell Samuelsson, right wing Rick Tocchet, and goaltender Ken Wregget. The trade added grit to the Pittsburgh lineup, but it didn't help morale. At the beginning of March, the Penguins met with Patrick to air their complaints with Bowman, who was blamed by some players for the trades.

There was one positive note. Mario scored his 1,000th NHL point on March 22 against Hartford in a 2–2 tie. It was his 513th game. Mario won the scoring title two weeks later with 133 points (in only 64 games), and Pittsburgh finished third in the Patrick Division.

Defensive Genius

In Games 3 and 4 of the 1992 playoff opening series against Washington, the Penguins scored eight goals (Mario had set up five and scored the other three). But still Washington led the series 3–1. Mario surprised everyone by suggesting a new defensive strategy: the one-deep forechecker system. He briefed the team, and Pittsburgh went on to win Game Five and take the series in seven games.

Washington coach Terry Murray said: "We were beaten by one man. Number 66. Lemieux."

WASHINGTON WON the first two games of their epic first-round series. Mario responded as he always does: he missed the first game, looked good in the second, and exploded in the third. In that 6–4 win, Mario set up the first three Pittsburgh goals and scored the next three.

After Washington won the next game 7–2, Mario suggested a new defensive system—one man deep on the forecheck. Bowman went along with the plan, Mario briefed the team, and the Penguins staved off elimination 5–2.

In a see-saw sixth game, Pittsburgh took a 2–0 lead, only to give up four straight Washington goals. Mario took over, playing two-thirds of the game and engineering or scoring four Pittsburgh goals to run up a total of five points. In five games, Mario now had 15 points.

The deciding game saw Mario score shorthanded and Jagr notch a power-play goal, the only scores the Penguins needed in a 3–1 series-clinching win.

Bowman's comment: "I have coached a lot of great players, but I have never seen a guy so inspired."

Pittsburgh now played the New York Rangers, the regular-season league champions. The Penguins won the first game 4–2, and early in the second the Rangers' Adam Graves slashed Mario on the left hand, breaking a bone. Mario was out for the series.

"We made something very bad work in our favor," Bowman said. Without Mario, the Penguins pulled together to stave off defeat, but the star's return brought a boost. "Beginning with the over-time win in game four against New York," Bowman's biographer wrote, "Bowman's Penguins won eleven consecutive playoff games, rolling over the Bruins in the conference finals and the Blackhawks . . . in the finals. In fifteen playoff games, Lemieux had scored 16 goals and contributed 18 assists." Five of those goals were game winners, tying an NHL playoff record and winning him his second consecutive Conn Smythe Trophy as the playoff MVP. Even though Mario thought Barrasso should have won it, this Smythe was more richly deserved than ever.

Mario was the league's leading scorer (for a third time) despite missing 16 games, and the leader of a club whose coach had died, that had rebelled against his replacement, and that was shaken by key lineup changes. Mario returned to the playoffs with a broken hand. And somehow he was not even among the three finalists for the Hart Trophy. This was the last time the voters for the NHL's individual awards ignored Mario's feats. He was about to become much more than a top scorer.

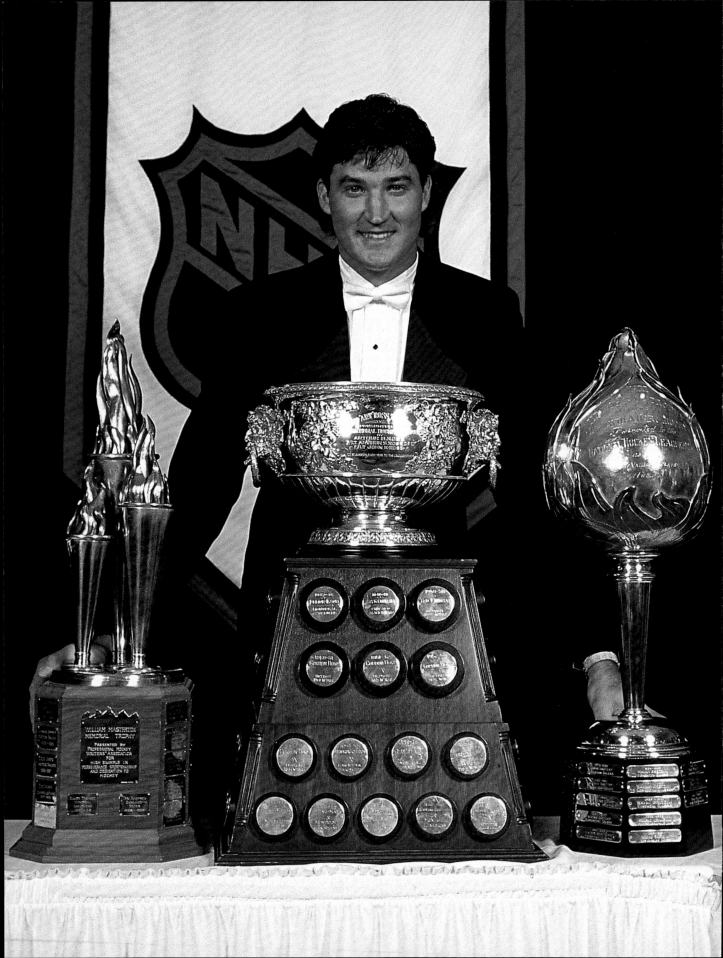

Sparkling silverware

from Le Magnifique's

unforgettable 1993

season: the Masterton

Memorial, Art Ross,

and Hart Trophies.

CHAPTER SEVEN

A Magnificent Season

IF EVER A repeat Stanley Cup winner looked
ready to cruise to a third, it was Pittsburgh.
Mario believed that during the 1992 playoffs the Penguins had become a team
"that could beat you any number of ways, using any number of styles. . . . Tighten
it up. Run and gun. Didn't really matter."

Mario had a new $42-million contract that paid six million dollars per sea-
son, plus money to be paid after his retirement. It was twice what Gretzky was
being paid. And Mario had what great scorers need most—Bowman gave him
all the ice time he wanted.

Playing with Kevin Stevens and Rick Tocchet, Mario scored 32 points in the
Penguins' first 10 games. Pittsburgh didn't lose until their 11th game, and lost

only two more of their first 20. After 16 games Mario had scored 21 goals and 46 points. The media began printing comparisons between Mario's scoring totals and Wayne Gretzky's record-setting seasons, and Mario talked about what it would take to beat those records:

"I think it's possible to score one hundred [goals]," he said. "For sure, you have to be on a roll. You can't go three or four games without scoring. You have to be consistent and get your goal every game and get four or five goals a couple of times."

As it happened, Gretzky was out of action with a herniated disc. The hockey world was Mario's oyster.

A FEW DAYS before Christmas, Mario mentioned to the Pittsburgh team doctor, Dr. Charles Burke, that he had a lump on his neck. It had been there about 18 months. The doctor thought he was looking at an enlarged lymph node, which when swollen due to infection becomes hard and tender. A small section of the node was removed for testing.

Just after Christmas, Mario's back started acting up again. That seemed to be worse news than the lump. But then the test results arrived, confirming that Mario had a form of cancer, Hodgkin's lymphoma. Mario knew that a cousin of his and two uncles had died of cancer.

Years later, Mario reflected, "When they told me I had Hodgkin's disease, it was probably the worst day of my life. I mean, everything was going so well.

"I cried on the way home from the doctor's office, cried when I told Nathalie, cried about my future."

He was leading the league with 104 points. Pittsburgh was in first place overall. The city was shocked that the man many believed was the greatest athlete ever to play in Pittsburgh was ill.

CAREFULLY CONTROLLED doses of radiation were aimed at the infected lymph node. Mario had 22 doses of radiation, sometimes day after day,

The Lemieux Foundation

In 1992–93, Mario Lemieux was diagnosed with Hodgkin's disease, a form of cancer. To support cancer treatment and research, he formed the Mario Lemieux Foundation, a charitable foundation that now also funds research into other medical conditions. The Austin Lemieux Neonatal Research Project, named after Mario's son who was born several months premature, supports research at a Pittsburgh women's hospital into pre-birth difficulties. The foundation also supports such organizations as a Pittsburgh center for artificial organ development, the Leukemia Society, the Lupus Foundation, and the Children's Hospital of Pittsburgh.

during February 1993. As the treatment went on, the side-effects got more painful, and Mario knew that they would get worse for a long period after the radiation ended.

While Mario was undergoing therapy, Pat LaFontaine, Mario's scoring rival 10 years before in the Quebec Major Junior Hockey League, became the NHL scoring leader, moving ahead of Mario by a dozen points. Early in the treatments Mario went to the NHL All-Star game, and told LaFontaine that he would be coming after him. Mario had missed 23 games.

Mario received one last big dose on March 2, which left a red burn mark on his neck. That night he played in Philadelphia, where he was honored with

a minute-and-a-half standing ovation. Mario played 21 minutes and scored a goal and an assist, adding up to what one sportswriter called not such a bad night's work, "considering Lemieux began the day as a cancer patient."

From then on Mario was playing with a shrinking energy pool. "I felt good until about the third week of radiation, when I started to get tired and couldn't eat because I was too sore. When I came back to the lineup after the treatments I felt a little bit tired, and then by the time the playoffs rolled around I didn't have any gas."

In March Mario played the most amazing stretch of games in a career that redefined greatness. He started out slowly, playing only five minutes against the Rangers because of back pain; had an assist in a win against Boston; and then was involved in all four goals in a 4–3 win over the Kings.

In 16 games running into early April, Mario scored 27 goals and 51 points. He scored four in each of two consecutive games. First, against Washington on March 18, Mario scored at one minute, then scored the next goal of the game, and went on to total six points in a 7–5 Pittsburgh win. It was their fourth-straight victory and it tied the Penguins with Montreal for first place overall. Two days later Mario scored four more goals against Phila-delphia, so that by March 20, he had sliced Lafontaine's scoring lead to 131–123, or eight points. Mario's second five-goal game of the season came against the Rangers in Pittsburgh's 16th-straight win.

Mario controls the puck

with his skate against the

Colorado Avalanche.

Mario beat LaFontaine for the Art Ross Trophy by the same dozen points he trailed him by on March 2. His 160 points in 60 games, extended over the 84-game schedule introduced that season, would have broken Gretzky's records.

As it was, Mario's cancer scare and bad back made him a hero to those who vote on the NHL's individual awards. Not only did he win his fourth Art Ross, but also the Hart Trophy and the Lester B. Pearson Award. Fittingly, he earned the Bill Masterton Memorial Trophy for "perseverance, sportsmanship, and dedication to hockey." As captain of the Penguins since 1987, Mario also led the club to the President's Trophy for the most points earned by a team during the regular season—a franchise record 56 games. It was the first time Pittsburgh had ever won it.

The team that reeled off 11 straight wins to take the Stanley Cup a year earlier, and 16 straight wins to end the season in playoff overdrive, survived only one playoff series, the one against New Jersey. Pittsburgh was called "unbeatable."

But the Penguins lost to the Islanders that spring in seven games. Mario's back forced him to leave Game One after two minutes, miss the next game, be on and off in the third, and be helped off the trainer's table as the Islanders tied the series. The medical staff tried putting him into traction, stretching his back—and it worked! Mario felt great, scored early, and Pittsburgh won Game Five. Mario played Game Six, but New York won. And the Islanders won the seventh game in overtime.

MARIO HAD HIS second major back operation on July 28. He played a career-low 22 games the following season, 1993–94. "It wasn't the back as much as it was fatigue from the radiation and the cancer," Mario has explained. To beat cancer, the disease has to become inactive and the patient has to recover from the effects of the treatment. Remarked Mario, "My stamina, which had always been there, wasn't the same. I wasn't able to perform." Pittsburgh lost the first playoff round in six games to Washington.

Mario sat out the 1994–95 season then came back stronger than ever. He lifted weights for the first time in his career and put in hundreds of miles on the stationary bike. He played his first 70-game season since 1989, scoring 69 goals for a career total of 561.

Pittsburgh finished first in the Northeast Division and beat archrivals Washington and the New York Rangers, before losing in seven games to that season's Cinderella club, the Florida Panthers.

Up to the last two weeks before the 1996–97 training camp, Mario was "99.9 percent sure" he would not play that season. "I thought my career was over." The Penguins' majority owner, Howard Baldwin, told Mario that, with him, Pittsburgh could win another Stanley Cup. After speaking with his wife, Nathalie, and his friends, Mario gave it one more try.

It was a frustrating season—Pittsburgh went 6–13–1 in the club's first 20 games—with a few more milestones for Mario. By the time he decided to retire at the end of the season, Mario had netted 613 goals, making him the sixth-leading goal scorer in NHL history.

Stairway to the Stars

During the 745 regular-season games Mario Lemieux played during his first NHL career, he surpassed the career goal-scoring totals of several hockey legends. Mario scored his 500th goal on October 26, 1995, against the New York Islanders.

Goal	Date of Mario's Goal	Legend	Games Played by Legend
508	November 10, 1995	Jean Beliveau	1,125
534	January 16, 1996	Frank Mahovlich	1,181
542	February 18, 1996	Stan Mikita	1,395
545	February 24, 1996	Maurice Richard	978
557	March 26, 1996	John Bucyk	1,540
561	April 10, 1996	Guy Lafleur	930
574	December 6, 1996	Mike Bossy	752
611	April 3, 1997	Bobby Hull	1,063

Au revoir but not

goodbye. Mario waves

to the crowd after

scoring his 70th

playoff goal in

his first Last Game.

CHAPTER EIGHT

The Player-Owner

THE PENGUINS were losing their opening-round playoff series against Philadelphia three games to none, so it looked as if Mario's last game on Pittsburgh ice would be April 23, 1997. True to his nature, Mario had made no farewell tour of the league—although there was a ceremony at the Montreal Forum, where the Canadiens' owners, the Molson family, saluted his final appearance in his hometown. For a superstar of Mario's stature, his goodbye to the NHL would be a low-key affair.

With five minutes left in the Philadelphia playoff game, though, the emotion burst through. Pittsburgh was winning 3–1, so the mood was right for a joyous farewell. For those final five minutes, the home crowd chanted *Mar*-io, *Mar*-io,

Mar-io. In the midst of the hubbub, Mario scored on a breakaway in the concluding minutes to seal a 4–1 victory and extend the series to a fifth game in Philadelphia.

The Pittsburgh public relations department made sure that Mario was named the game's number one star. Instead of taking his usual two-step twirl, Mario set out on a final lap around the rink. "It was totally spontaneous.... I decided to go around the rink and thank the fans for a lot of great memories in 13 years. That was probably the first time I ever cried on the ice."

Pittsburgh lost in Philadelphia, so Mario's first NHL career came to an end three days later, on the road, with Mario embracing heir-apparent Eric Lindros in the postgame handshake lineup.

November 17, 1997, Mario was inducted into the Hockey Hall of Fame. The usual three-year waiting period was dropped, an honor later extended to Wayne Gretzky as well. Mario was accompanied into the Hall by Bryan Trottier, who won four Stanley Cups with the Islanders and two more with Pittsburgh, and Glen Sather, mastermind of five Cup-winning Oiler teams. Four days later, Mario's Number 66 was retired and elevated into the dome of the building then known as Pittsburgh's Civic Arena. And that, it seemed, was that.

MARIO'S IDEA of retirement was to play golf, spend time with his young family, and "get up in the morning not knowing what to expect," as he put it in his autobiography, *The Final Period.* "I just want to try it for one year and see if I like it.

"If not? Then I'm going to look for work."

Instead, work found him. By the fall of 1999 the Pittsburgh Penguins faced bankruptcy.

The money the club owed him in deferred payments was at risk. That September Mario acquired about 35 percent of the Penguins for $5 million cash and $20 million of the money the club owed him in deferred payments. Two-and-a-half years after that game in Philadelphia, Mario was back in the NHL— as the principal owner of the Penguins. Having saved the franchise as a player by leading it to two

Mario's Subpar Game

When Mario Lemieux was 17 years old, his former agent, Bob Perno, introduced him to golf. Perno took Mario and his older brother, Alain, to play at St. Hyacinthe; Mario shot 116, a good first-time score. "After a few times out," Lawrence Martin writes in *Mario,* "he was breaking 100. Within a year, he was breaking 80. Within a few years, he was breaking par." Today Mario is a long-hitting scratch (zero handicap) golfer who plays several tournaments a year. Now if only hockey didn't interfere with his tee times.

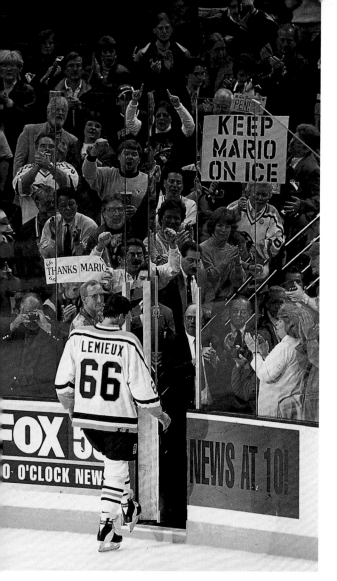

Stanley Cups, he rescued it again by buying it. In Mario's first year as principal owner the club turned $16 million in losses into a small profit.

Then on December 8, 2000, Mario told the Penguins that he would be returning. He suited up to play his first game on December 27 against the Toronto Maple Leafs. And though he slipped into retirement without much fanfare, hockey fans were set to celebrate his return with style.

Comeback day started for Mario with a good night's sleep, his wife, Nathalie, told a sportscaster who asked her that very question during the Pittsburgh–Toronto second period, when Mario had already scored three points, Pittsburgh led 5–0, and any moment of his day so far seemed newsworthy. He had been nervous, Mario allowed, as he usually was before big games. Around noon, dressed in a dark suit and tie, he left for work. On this special occasion, a television camera recorded the moment. In the large, wood-paneled foyer of the traditional brick Lemieux house in the exclusive Pittsburgh suburb of Sewickley, Mario said goodbye to two of his three daughters, Lauren, seven, and Stephanie, five (the third, Alexa, was three), turned to his son Austin, four, bent down, offered his hand, and said, "Alright, give me five, Buddy!"

Stephanie piped up, "Let's go to the hockey game *now*...."

She was two when Mario retired from hockey, so Stephanie might never have known that for 13 years her father usually left for the rink several hours before games.

"In a little bit," Nathalie Lemieux told Stephanie.

That evening 17,148 fans packed Pittsburgh's Mellon Arena to witness history in the making. Before the game, they watched as the black, gold, and white banner emblazoned with "Lemieux 66 1984–1997" was slowly lowered from the dome, taking a full two minutes to make its graceful descent, and Tina

Turner's voice boomed from the loudspeakers singing "The Best." The overflow crowd cheered the entire time.

Nathalie and Austin stood by the center-ice boards, eyes upturned, as the banner arrived at ice level. Eyes like saucers, mouth wide open, Austin, *People* magazine reported, "looked as if he had just seen Santa Claus." Mario said that one reason for his comeback was so that Austin, his only son, born three months premature 45 days before his first retirement, could see his dad play. Watching the game that night, Austin was just a little older than Mario had been when he started taking hockey lessons.

Within seconds of the faceoff, Mario showed that he was back. His 1,495th National Hockey League point—"Mario Lemieux's first point in 1,340 days," *Hockey Night in Canada*'s color man Harry Neale cracked—was one of those gifts from the hockey gods that set Mario Lemieux apart. It was a true playmaker's goal, a play most NHLers wouldn't even try. Instead of bringing the puck out in front of the net, Mario just shot it into the confusion. It hit Leafs defenseman Danny Markov's skates and bounced around, evading Curtis Joseph's frantic glove. And it slid free at the moment Jaromir Jagr arrived at the net. The video replay didn't really make clear which had entered the net first, Jagr or the puck.

The officials' decision allowing the goal to stand was a close call. It could have gone either way. But Mario, on the scoreboard after 33 seconds of his comeback, sent a message. Mario was back. Even at 35, he was the same old Mario.

HIS RETURN STANDS alone in professional sports. It has happened twice before that members of the Hockey Hall of Fame played again in the NHL. Gordie Howe had a 25-season NHL career, interrupted by a four-year retirement and six seasons in the World Hockey Association before he returned to the NHL with Hartford for 1979–80. And Mario's hero, Canadiens great Guy Lafleur, enjoyed a brief comeback with the Rangers and Quebec after a three-year retirement. But Mario retired, not as a

Hired Hand

As unique as it may seem for Mario Lemieux to own and play for the Pittsburgh Penguins, at least two owners of professional hockey clubs have played for their teams before. Frank and Lester Patrick (and their father Joe) founded and owned the Pacific Coast Hockey Association for 15 years, during which Frank played defense for the Stanley Cup–winning Vancouver Millionaires in 1915. Lester played for Victoria of the PCHA. But player-owners are rare. Mario is the first in the National Hockey League.

player in decline, but as the NHL scoring champion. No player at his level, in any sport, has returned to play as well as when he left. Never in modern times has a player come back as owner of the team he played for.

The business logic of his return soon became obvious: Pittsburgh sold out all 24 games after Mario's comeback, generating $3.5 million more in revenue. He was also making money for clubs Pittsburgh played on the road; nearly all of his away games sold out as well.

Pittsburgh's "owner-operator," as *Sports Illustrated* labeled Mario, had become, once again, just one of the guys, hanging out in the dressing room, kidding and being kidded. Teammate Alexei Kovalev, called the hottest player in hockey at the time of Mario's comeback, was showing his goal-scoring moves to a sportscaster in Madison Square Garden's visitors' dressing room. As Kovalev removed items of equipment, he became more and more excited, explaining in Russian-accented English what he looked for from the goalie, and what he did in response. Just then, a teammate chirped, "He doesn't know."

The voice was Mario Lemieux's. "He's making it up!"

Kovalev ignored him. With an imaginary stick, Kovalev deked left, then deked right....

On the bench, Mario seemed to be having more fun than he ever had before playing hockey. In just over half the games, Mario scored almost two-thirds the points of Jaromir Jagr, who, playing on Mario's line, had returned to the NHL scoring leadership. Mario was actually smiling on the bench.

Proud father Mario with the most important reason for his comeback, son Austin.

There was another difference between Mario's first and second careers. When Mario joined the Penguins in 1984, Wayne Gretzky was about to record the third of his four 200-point seasons and the sixth of eight consecutive (and total of eleven) scoring titles. The year after Mario retired for the first time, the Great One led the NHL in assists.

When Gretzky retired in 1999, hockey fans wondered who would seize the torch of hockey greatness. Eric Lindros had been called the Next One. Young stars such as Joe Sakic and Paul Kariya were mentioned. Some picked Jaromir Jagr. It never occurred to anyone that the 35-year-old Mario Lemieux might be the next one.

S T A T I S T I C S

Quebec Major Junior Hockey League (QMJHL)

Regular Season

Year	Team	GP	G	A	P	PIM
1981–82	Laval	64	30	66	96	22
1982–83	Laval	66	84	100	184	76
1983–84	Laval	70	133*	149*	282*	92
Totals		**200**	**247**	**315**	**562**	**190**

Playoffs

Year	Team	GP	G	A	P	PIM
1982	Laval	18	5	9	14	31
1983	Laval	12	14	18	32	18
1984	Laval	14	29*	23*	52*	29
Totals		**44**	**48**	**50**	**98**	**78**

National Hockey League (NHL)

Regular Season

Year	Team	GP	G	A	P	PIM
1984–85	Pittsburgh	73	43	57	100	54
1985–86	Pittsburgh	79	48	93	141	43
1986–87	Pittsburgh	63	54	53	107	57
1987–88	Pittsburgh	77	70	98*	168*	92
1988–89	Pittsburgh	76	85*	114*	199*	100
1989–90	Pittsburgh	59	45	78	123	78
1990–91	Pittsburgh	26	19	26	45	30
1991–92	Pittsburgh	64	44	87	131*	94
1992–93	Pittsburgh	60	69	91	160*	38
1993–94	Pittsburgh	22	17	20	37	32
1994–95	Did not play					
1995–96	Pittsburgh	70	69*	92*	161*	54
1996–97	Pittsburgh	76	50	72*	122*	65
2000–01	Pittsburgh	43	35	41	76	18
Totals		**788**	**648**	**922**	**1570**	**755**

Playoffs

Year	Team	GP	G	A	P	PIM
1989	Pittsburgh	11	12	7	19	16
1991	Pittsburgh	23	16	28*	44*	16
1992	Pittsburgh	15	16*	18	34*	2
1993	Pittsburgh	11	8	10	18	10
1994	Pittsburgh	6	4	3	7	2
1996	Pittsburgh	18	11	16	27	33
1997	Pittsburgh	5	3	3	6	4
2001	Pittsburgh	18	6	11	17	4
Totals		**107**	**76**	**96**	**172**	**87**

International hockey

Year	Event	GP	G	A	P	PIM
1983	World Juniors	7	5	5	10	12
1985	World Championships	9	4	6	10	2
1987	Rendez-Vous	2	0	3	3	0
1987	Canada Cup	9	11	7	18	8

Awards

Year	Award
1984	Canadian Major Junior Player of the Year
1985	Calder Memorial Trophy (NHL rookie of the year)
1986, 87, 92	NHL Second All-Star Team
1986, 88, 93, 96	Lester B. Pearson Award (NHL MVP, as voted by the players)
1988, 93, 96	Hart Trophy (NHL MVP, as voted by the press)
1988, 89, 92, 93, 96, 97	Art Ross Trophy (NHL top point scorer)
1988, 89, 93, 96, 97	NHL First All-Star Team
1991, 92	Conn Smythe Trophy (NHL playoff MVP)
1993	Bill Masterton Memorial Trophy (dedication to hockey)
1993	Alka-Seltzer Plus Award (excellence in plus-minus standings)

Played in the NHL All-star game in 1985–86, 88–90, 92, 96–97, 2001

Key

GP = Games Played   G = Goals   A = Assists   P = Points
PIM = Penalties in Minutes   * League-leading total

jB
LEMIEUX

Rossiter, Sean.

Mario Lemieux.

$12.95

BAKER & TAYLOR